There are high spots
in all of our lives
and most of them
have come about through
encouragement
from someone else.

I don't care how great,
how famous or successful
a man or woman may be,
each hungers for
applause.

George M. Adams

180 Ways to WALK the Recognition TALK

The "How To" Handbook
For
EVERYONE

Eric Harvey

To order additional copies of
180 Ways To Walk The Recognition Talk
or for information on other
WALK THE TALK® products and services
contact us at
1.888.822.9255
or visit our website at
www.walkthetalk.com

WALKTHETALK.COM

Resources for Personal and Professional Success

Printed in the United States of America
20 19 18 17 16 15 14 13 12 11

Printed by MultiAd

ISBN 1-885228-36-8

90000

9 781885 228369

*D*edicated...

...to the three women in my life
Nancy, Nicole, and Erika
who have recognized me with their unconditional love.

*T*hank you...

...to the entire
WALK THE TALK® Company Team

with *special* thanks and recognition to
Steve Ventura
for his encouragement, editing expertise, and
many valuable contributions to this resource.

*S*ome people call it "positive reinforcement." Others, a "motivational strategy." Still others label it "common courtesy" – a sign of appreciation. But most folks refer to it as "RECOGNITION." And it's one of the biggest *un*kept secrets in business today!

Why an "*un*kept secret"? Well, there's certainly no shortage of research and expert opinion on the positive impacts of recognition in the workplace. Fact is, recognition fosters job satisfaction, builds self-esteem, and reinforces desired performance. It supports quality, strengthens trust and loyalty, and helps shape a "magnetic" culture that attracts and keeps the very best people. Yet, despite these (and a lot more) widely accepted and well-documented benefits, far too many recognition opportunities are being missed in far too many organizations, every day. And chances are you're both a victim *of* and contributor *to* this reality.

Here's a short, two-question survey that you'll probably be able to answer without investing much think time:

1. Ever feel unappreciated or under recognized for the good work you do?
2. Ever miss opportunities to recognize the people you work with (direct reports, peers, AND bosses) for the good work that they do?

If you're like most folks, there's a good chance your two answers were DUH! and OOPS! (a.k.a., yes and yes). Of course, all of us occasionally feel taken for granted. We know firsthand how lousy that feels. And when we fail to *give* the recognition our co-workers desire, we pass along that same lousy feeling. We do it not because we're bad people, but because we're human ... and we sometimes lose sight of what's truly important.

But we all have an opportunity to change that.

First, we need to get past a couple of fairly common <u>fallacies</u>: 1) that recognition is a touchy-feely, warm-fuzzy thing that "sensitive types" do, and 2) that giving recognition is solely management's responsibility. WRONG and WRONG AGAIN! Recognition is about acknowledging good results and reinforcing positive performance; it's about shaping an environment in which contributions are noticed and appreciated. And that's a responsibility shared by EVERYONE!

Next, we need to understand that there are personal benefits to be gained by recognizing others; there *IS* something in it for each of us. We not only feel good by making others feel good, but we also improve our own lot by encouraging the positive attitudes and behaviors that eventually make life easier for us. And don't forget "The Law of Reciprocity": *What Goes Around COMES around!*

Finally, we need guidelines, ideas, and suggestions on HOW to recognize others.

That's what this handbook is all about.

As you read on, you'll find a collection of (180, to be exact) simple yet powerful techniques, strategies, practical "how to's," creative ideas, and a few things to remember – all designed to help you do an even better job of recognizing others.

Will every one of the 180 ideas presented fit your particular situation? Of course not! No book could make that claim. But not to worry. You'll find more than enough information here to attain recognition's ultimate goal:

to bring out the best in others ... and the best in you!

*G*etting started
How to use this handbook.

180 Ways To Walk The Recognition Talk is jam-packed with techniques, strategies, "how to's," and things to remember. In fact, there's *so* much good information, it might be a little difficult figuring out how to use it all. Here are a few suggestions to get you started:

First, read the handbook from cover to cover with a highlighter in hand. Mark any key words or phrases that you find particularly relevant and meaningful.

Next, select three ideas or action items that you wish to personally adopt. Circle the number of each item you select (1-180) and mark the pages they appear on with "sticky notes." Review those pages frequently.

Finally, each time you complete/master one of your action items, draw an "X" through its circled number and select a new item to work on in its place. That way, you'll have three ideas working at all times. Before you know it, your handbook will be filled with crossed-out numbers … and you'll be well on your way to

walking the recognition talk.

*C*ontents

Starting with the basics ... 1

Top 10 Excuses for *NOT* Giving Recognition ... 8

Expanding the possibilities ... 11

A Letter to Every Manager ... 15

Going "outside the box" ... 25

A Note to Every Employee ... 32

Recognition Checklist ... 39

A *Soldier*
will fight long and hard
for a bit of
colored ribbon.

Napoleon Bonaparte

Starting with the basics

*A ppreciative words
are the most powerful force for good
on earth!*

–George W. Crane

1. Remember that gimmicks, gadgets, and giveaways can make your recognition efforts fun and memorable. But nothing (I mean NOTHING!) can replace a good, old-fashioned, sincere, look-'em-in-the-eye-and-say "thank you."

2. LEND AN EAR! Looking for a really low-cost way to recognize others? Try *listening* to them! Listening is one of the most underutilized recognition activities in the world. (And one of the most underdeveloped skills!) But it can have a big impact. Whether a person is a peer, a direct report, a boss, or a customer, listening to them sends the message that you care … and that they are important!

3. GET PHYSICAL! Make a habit of using positive, non-verbal recognition gestures like "thumbs up" or "high fives." These simple actions not only recognize others, but also help spread contagious enthusiasm throughout the workplace.

4. Remember the "Platinum Rule": Recognize others the way *they* want to be recognized. Don't assume that others appreciate the same forms of praise that you do. Successful recognition is in the eye of the receiver, not the giver!

5. Here's a question to ask new folks who join your team: "When you do a good job, how do you like to be recognized?" You'll not only learn about what motivates people, but you'll also begin establishing an expectation that team members *will* do a good job! This great "double hit" technique really is effective.

6. Here's a lesson from HUMAN NATURE 101 to remember and apply in your dealings with everyone in your organization: Behaviors that get reinforced get repeated. You can take THAT to the bank!

7. KNOW THEM AS PEOPLE! Find out what's important to the folks you work with. Ask about hobbies, favorite sports, ideal vacations, family, etc. This shows that you're interested in *who* they are in life rather than just *what* they are at work. That's recognition at its most basic level!

8. BE ACCESSIBLE! Make time for the people you work with – especially those that work *for* you. The more attention you pay, the more important they'll feel.

9. HELP THEM GROW! Work with people to develop their talents and enhance their skills. When you put time, energy, and resources into others' development, you not only recognize their potential, but you also "set them up" for future success.

10. Here are a few things you can "give" people to recognize their importance and contributions: respect, responsibility, honesty, feedback, trust, and cooperation. Sound familiar? Chances are these or similar attributes can be found in your organizational values. So, let your values be your guide. Sometimes the most meaningful recognition comes from just "walking the talk."

11. CELEBRATE SUCCESS! Consider closing meetings and training sessions with discussions about people who exhibit the positive behaviors your organization says are important. Who has recently delivered superior customer service? Who is a role model when it comes to teamwork? Who has made a valuable contribution that deserves our thanks? Ask these questions regularly. You'll find more than enough positive examples!

12. You can increase the impact of your recognition by linking performance to "big picture" end states. Rather than just saying, "Wow, you really handled that well," try something like: "What you did really enhanced our relationship with a very important client. I'm convinced she will do business with us again soon. And you're a big reason for that."

13. Start to develop an "attitude of gratitude" by creating a written list of performance and behaviors deserving of recognition. Put down everything you can think of. Add to the list periodically. Most importantly, keep an eye out for people who do things on your list and recognize them! Here are 10 recognition opportunities to get your list started:

- Long-term positive performance such as perfect attendance for a year.
- Exceeding expectations, like coming in under budget.
- Volunteering for a tough assignment.
- Helping others in the organization meet *their* goals.
- Displaying "contagious enthusiasm" on the job.
- Submitting a cost- or time-saving idea.
- Requesting/accepting additional responsibilities.
- Going "above and beyond" for a customer.
- Successful completion of an in-house training course or outside continuous education program.
- Keeping a cool head under pressure.

14. Be observant of surroundings. When you visit someone's work area, pay attention to pictures, mementos, etc., that they have around. You can bet that anything displayed is important to them. Ask questions like: "Who are these children in the picture?" or "Would you mind telling me about this award?" You'll show your interest in the person, AND you'll get somewhat of a read on what types of recognition are important to them.

15. Here's a biggie: FOCUS ON STRENGTHS more than you focus on individual weaknesses. Use the "80/20 Rule": Spend 80% of your time reinforcing what's going right and only 20% of your time trying to fix what's wrong. Fact is, most of the time things do go right. And the attention you pay ought to reflect that.

16. THE LAST TIME? Make a list of all the people who work with or for you. Then go through your list and identify the last time you gave recognition to each person … and for what. You should remember your last praising of most of the people on the list. If not, **you're probably not doing it enough!**

> *Everyone has an invisible sign*
> *   hanging from their neck saying,*
> *"Make me feel important."*
>
> Mary Kay Ash

17. Looking to encourage recognition and build a culture of appreciation? **Try giving recognition for giving recognition!** Think about it: Since reinforced behavior is repeated behavior, if you praise those who praise others, they'll be motivated to do it even more. Others will see this and *they'll* join in. Before you know it, EVERYBODY will be doing it! What a problem!

18. MAKE IT SINCERE! Probably the number one characteristic of good recognition is *sincerity*. Most people will be able to tell when you really mean what you say and when you're "just going through the motions." And if you ask folks, they'll usually agree that insincere recognition is worse than none at all. Chances are that you feel the same way, right?

Okay, so how *can* you "be" sincere? Look them in the eyes and tell them what their good performance means to you personally; tell them how it makes you feel! If you really do appreciate the good work of others, it will shine through. If you don't appreciate it, you need to do some serious soul searching to find out why!

19. BE SPECIFIC! The more specific your recognition, the more impact it will have. Instead of merely saying, "Great job," tell the person what it was about the job that was done so well. Example: "That was terrific work. You came in under budget, you completed the work six days ahead of schedule, and you had everyone working together as a team. I really appreciate your efforts and your results." When you're specific, the person knows exactly what behaviors to replicate in the future.

20. MAKE IT TIMELY! Recognition loses impact with the passing of time. Receiving praise for something you did many months ago is not all that motivating and can feel contrived. A good rule of thumb: Give recognition as soon as possible after the positive behavior or performance.

21. If you give group (team) recognition, follow it up with individual recognition for specific contributions. Take any group activity and you'll find that some people work harder and contribute more than others. And they know it! When you recognize everyone equally, you run the risk of turning off your superior performers.

(See checklist on page 39)

22. WHY? ASK WHY! When someone gives YOU recognition, try to find out the "why" behind the acknowledgment. Ask for specifics that will help you zero in on your strengths … and use them more often.

23. KEEP IT PROPORTIONAL! Make sure the amount and type of recognition given is appropriate for the behavior being recognized. Performance at the "curing cancer" level obviously deserves more than a verbal *thank you*. But a simple "pat on the back" might be appropriate for one year of perfect attendance. This more than any other characteristic requires good judgment.

24. Here's another one you can take to the bank: Bosses need and want praise, too! Far too often, recognition is seen as something *they* (supervisors and managers) are supposed to do for *them* (employees). Fact is, we ALL need positive reinforcement! And there's no better way for a leader to know that he or she is doing a good job than to hear it from those being led.

You __earn the right__ to expect recognition by giving it! It's that simple.

25. DON'T FORGET YOUR PEERS! How often do you recognize your co-workers? If not all that often, why not? Whenever one person performs well or makes a contribution, *everyone* benefits in some way. Why not thank people for carrying their share of the load? Why not show appreciation when others make your work unit (and you) look good?

26. Be sure to give recognition to your "middle stars" – those day-in and day-out solid performers who keep the business going. They represent the vast majority of your organization … and a huge recognition opportunity zone. Avoid the trap of giving most of your attention to "super stars" (exceptional performers) and "fallen stars" (those with performance problems).

27. DIVERSIFY! Don't get in a rut giving the same kind of recognition all the time. Mix it up. Use a variety of verbal "atta boys," written commendations, awards, perks, etc. You'll make it more meaningful for the receivers and a lot more fun for you!

28. THINK STANLEY CUP – the trophy given to the winner of the National Hockey League championship. Each member of the winning team is given the trophy for two days so they can "show it off" to (and celebrate with) their family and hometown fans. How can you replicate the power of that practice?

29. Recognize the "behind the scenes" people that help "sell" your organization. For example, praise the accounts receivable clerk who enhanced your relationship with a slow-paying customer, or celebrate the positive comment you received from a vendor about your attentive receptionist.

30. If you provide tangible rewards for outstanding performance, allow "rewardees" to choose between a few options. Not everyone appreciates football tickets; some people wouldn't be caught dead wearing a printed t-shirt.

31. CHECK YOUR FACTS! Make sure people truly deserve praise before you give it. The only thing worse than insincere recognition is *unearned* recognition – especially when it's seen by others who know what's really going on.

32. Use formal awards and recognition programs existing in your organization whenever appropriate. Nominate worthy candidates every chance you get! Just remember that these are only the tip of the recognition iceberg. Even if you don't have access to (or control of) such formal processes, there are literally hundreds of things you can do to acknowledge positive performance. You'll find 148 more of them as you read on.

Top 10 Excuses for *NOT* Giving Recognition

(with opinionated responses)

1. "I don't know how."

No doubt this can be an honest and valid concern. Most folks never receive any type of training on giving recognition. That's the very reason for writing this handbook. So use the material you find in these pages.

2. "I don't have time."

For sure, time is a precious and limited resource. Most of us have more stuff to do than time to do it in. But somehow we all manage to do the things that are *really* important to us. So, if you feel you don't have time to recognize others, it may be that you just haven't made it a high enough priority. Besides, how much time does it take to say, "Thank you" or "I appreciate it"?

3. "People don't care about it all that much."

Yeah, right! Okay, if you look hard enough, maybe you can find one or two people who couldn't give a flip about being recognized. And you can probably find a handful who *say* it's not important to them. But for every person like that, there are hundreds who like being stroked for their efforts and contributions. Play the odds!

4. "It's not MY job!"

Think that giving recognition is strictly a top-down thing that only "bosses" are responsible for? THINK AGAIN! That's a fallacy – and it's one of the biggest reasons why recognition doesn't happen as often as it could ... and should. Fact is, supporting an environment in which people are acknowledged and truly appreciated is *everyone's* job. To believe otherwise is to assume that only supervisors need be concerned with basic courtesy.

5. *"I don't believe in rewarding people for just doing their job!"*

Me neither! A "reward" is something special and should be reserved for special achievement. But recognition is different. It's an acknowledgment, a favorable notice, and a reinforcement that increases the likelihood that people will keep doing their jobs ... and making work that much easier for *you*!

6. *"It becomes meaningless if done too much."*

Maybe so, but most organizations have a looooooong way to go before the meter reads "Too Much Recognition Happening Here." Actually, it's insincerity rather than quantity that tends to devalue recognition.

7. *"I'm very limited in what I can do."*

Chances are that you're limited mostly by untapped imagination. Okay, so you don't control or even have access to money and formal award programs. Those only represent the tip of the recognition iceberg, anyway. Get creative! You'll find plenty of low-cost, informal recognition examples in this book. Develop more.

8. *"Sometimes it's awkward and uncomfortable."*

So was the first time you drove a stick shift! But the more you did it, the easier it got (hopefully). And the more you liked doing it! If you're uncomfortable with recognition, there's a good chance you're not doing it enough. Go forth and PRACTICE!

9. *"People will think they've 'made it' and stop working hard."*

NOT! Think about it: Do *you* slow down when others show appreciation for your contributions? Enough said on this one.

10. *"I don't get it. Why should I give it?"*

Pure and simply because it's the right thing to do! You know how it feels to have your efforts and achievements overlooked. You know how it feels to be taken for granted. It stinks! Don't let one wrong become your rationale for doing another.

33. Write the word "recognition" in your calendar/day planning system at some regular interval (like every Friday for the entire year). Make this word your trigger to quickly think of people who deserve praise. Then, immediately go thank them for their positive performance. Trust me, if you make an effort to look, you'll never run out of people to praise.

34. Do you supervise other supervisors? If so, consider making "recognizing others" a performance expectation for them. Discuss it during coaching sessions and performance reviews. Require your supervisors to identify how they are contributing to a culture of appreciation. Remember that people tend to do what's *EX*pected when it's *IN*spected!

35. KEEP YOUR FINGER ON THE PULSE! Include questions on climate surveys and exit interviews that help you monitor the quantity and quality of your recognition activities.

36. We're all creatures of habit. Repeat an action enough times and it becomes habitual – an unconscious behavior. Here's a worthwhile habit to work on developing: Each day, "catch" at least one person doing something good … and praise them. Over time, you'll acquire a natural tendency to focus on the good stuff!

37. Remember that people's perceptions are their realities. Regardless of your good intentions and accompanying actions, the folks you work with are recognized only when they *feel* they are. It's not enough to focus merely on what *you do*, you've also got to be concerned with what *they think* (about what you do).

Expanding
the possibilities

> *r. Scorpio says productivity is up 2%, and it's all because of my motivational techniques, like donuts – and the possibility of more donuts to come!*
>
> –Homer Simpson

38. Become a RECOGNITION CATALYST! Once you find a person to recognize, pass the information on to a senior manager to add their personal message. With few exceptions, the person being recognized will appreciate acknowledgment from "Mr./Ms. Big." And the senior manager will no doubt appreciate the opportunity to recognize a valuable employee.

39. Give out "Certificates of Recognition." You can find blank forms in many office supply catalogs and motivational product stores. You can even buy certificate-making computer software. Put the certificates in inexpensive frames before presenting them.

40. USE *THEIR* HEAD! Develop recognition stickers and pins that people can wear on hard hats and caps. And consider having special head gear (e.g., gold in color) made up as recognition for special achievements.

41. Do you have a customer visiting you in the near future? Use the visit as an opportunity to recognize someone in your work group. Have the employee give the customer a tour, answer questions, and even join you for lunch. Being chosen to represent the group is a powerful form of recognition.

42. PUT THE CART BEFORE THE HORSE! Every once in a while, recognize someone BEFORE you know their specific accomplishment. Go up to the person and say, "I know you've done something this week deserving of recognition. What do you feel that is?"

43. WRITE THEM UP! Community editors of local newspapers are always looking for interesting stories. Why not let them write about the achievements of people in your work group? This unique form of recognition may be just a phone call away!

44. Want to recognize a team or group that consistently performs well? Consider buying some exercise equipment (e.g., stair stepper, stationary bike) and a small, portable stereo or "jam box" and set them up in an unused work area. This creates a real win/win! Not only are you providing a place to "de-stress" during the day, you're also promoting health and well-being.

45. MAKE AN APPOINTMENT to give recognition. For example: Ask someone, "What's a good time tomorrow for me to give you some positive feedback?" This *let it simmer* strategy increases the recognition impact, gives the employee something to look forward to, and shows that you respect his or her time.

46. ALLOW ME TO INTRODUCE YOURSELF! Seize every opportunity to introduce people in your work group to customers, visitors, vendors, "big wigs," etc. The message to your co-workers is, "You're important ... I want people to meet you." Pound for pound, introductions may be the most effective no-cost recognition you can give.

47. LEAVE RECOGNITION VOICE MAILS! Don't let being away on business (or being too busy) be an excuse for not recognizing a deserving person.

48. Tell someone how PROUD you are: to work with them, to have them as a boss, to be their supervisor, etc.

> A personal note to any macho men (or women) out there who may think this is a wimpy move:
> Let me take you back 30 years to when I was in the army. My platoon had accomplished a particular task extremely well. Our sergeant (picture a 250-lb., bulldog-looking, tough-skinned "lifer") called us together and said, "What you @$%&#s just did makes me PROUD to be in the same army." I've never forgotten his words – especially the word "proud."

49. POST THE RESULTS! Use charts, graphs, and posters to visually display positive group performance. Place them in common areas for everyone to see. And make sure each team member's name is included somewhere on each posting.

50. Add "Shameless Bragging" as a short agenda item to all staff or team meetings. Encourage participants to brag about someone who has had a positive impact on your customers, your culture, and of course, your bottom line.

51. TEACH BUSINESS LITERACY – the financial aspects of running a successful operation. Teaching people "the business of business" not only demonstrates that they are important members of the team, but it also helps build skills that can benefit the entire organization.

52. SHARE INFORMATION! Another underutilized and inexpensive recognition strategy is the sharing of non-confidential information – especially organizational performance data. So go up to someone you want to recognize, hand them a copy of the latest report (or memo, or whatever), and say: "You continually prove yourself to be an important member of our team. I'm including you on the routing list for this information so you'll be more aware of what's happening and how we're doing."

53. NOTIFY THE FAMILY! Send a letter or card to the person's family describing her/his performance and the positive impact it has on the organization. Close with something like: "We're very proud of Barbara ... you should be, too."

54. While we're on the subject of family, why not THANK A FAMILY MEMBER? Send a note, card, flowers, cookies, etc. Describe your co-worker's achievement and thank the spouse and/or other family members for their "behind the scenes" contributions. Support at home plays a big part in success at work.

55. "Let them eat cake!" Seriously, bringing goodies (food) to work is a great way to show people you appreciate their efforts. Whether you're a team member buying morning bagels, or a manager springing for pizza, remember that the road to recognition often passes through our stomachs.

56. If the person you're recognizing appreciates public praise, initiate A STANDING OVATION at your next gathering. S.O.'s are special and memorable ... and rare.

I've always been a sucker for attention!

Cuba Gooding, Jr.

57. Personally deliver a bouquet of balloons to the person's work location or have it waiting for them when they arrive.

58. Send an e-mail commendation and "cc" EVERYONE!

59. Recognize your positive performers by asking them to be teachers or mentors. Perhaps the ultimate acknowledgment of one's capacities and accomplishments is to be asked to teach and train others.

A Letter to Every Manager

Dear Boss:

Okay, maybe I've been known to say: "I don't want any pats on the back – just put it in my check." Well, don't believe it. It's a crock! Regardless of how I may act, I do care a lot about what you and others think of me and what I do. Recognition is important to me. That's why I wear award pins and belt buckles; that's why I display trophies at home; that's why I hang certificates on my wall.

Believe it or not, I'm looking for more from this job than just a paycheck. There's got to be more, 'cause I'm sure not gonna get rich on what I make! What do I want? I want to feel good about myself and the work I do; I want to feel like I'm an important part of this organization. And I tend to gauge my self-worth by others' perceptions ... including yours.

I don't expect you to see me as a top-notch performer all the time. No one is. But I do expect to occasionally be recognized for my efforts and contributions. And the more you recognize my good work, the more good work I want to do. That's "human nature."

I know you're often so busy you probably don't think about recognizing me. And maybe you sometimes figure that you don't get recognition yourself, so why should you give it to others? But if you'll just make a greater effort to let me know you appreciate me, I'll do my best to return the favor. And I promise I won't complain about receiving too much praise!

Every Employee

Adapted from *Walk Awhile In MY Shoes* by Eric Harvey and Steve Ventura

60. Invite a VIP (senior manager, key customer, local dignitary, etc.) to have a short visit with "the best organization in the area."

61. Buy a work-enhancing product that will benefit everyone and link its purchase to someone deserving of recognition. "Because of our project engineer, Juli Jones, and her cost-savings efforts on the ABC Project, we've been able to purchase a new widget maker for the department. This new machine will make all of our jobs easier. We have Juli to thank for that."

62. SEND THEM (or take them with you) TO A CONFERENCE. And when they return, ask them to give a short, informal briefing for everyone in your work group. This not only can be additional recognition for the attendee, but it can also increase the event's return on investment by "spreading the learning."

63. Get a **LEG** up on recognition:

> **L**ook them in the eye
> **E**xplain specifically what they did well
> **G**ive them a great big "Thank You!"

64. Help others develop a recognition mind-set. Display a large calendar with important dates noted such as employment anniversaries, birthdays, special personal events, etc.

65. GIVE 'EM A NEW MUG! (No we're not talking facelifts here!) Give imprinted or hand-painted coffee mugs as recognition pieces. They're practical, and the recognition is long lasting.

66. "TELL" ON A CO-WORKER! When you see someone do something that's worthy of recognition, do your part to make it happen: Tell the boss! Supervisors can't possibly be everywhere and see everything. They'll appreciate your observations of positive performance. And if *you're* the supervisor, make sure your people know that you WANT them to tell you about the good things that others do.

67. Arrange for a special thank you (note, letter, card, call, whatever!) to a deserving individual from your entire team, an internal customer group, clients, or the boss's boss's boss.

68. Keep a supply of "Thanks for a Job Well Done" (or similar message) cards handy at all times so you can strike while the recognition iron is hot. Set a personal goal to give out as many well-deserved cards as possible during the next 12 months.

69. Link a specific group recognition event to a specific business goal. For example, you might make a team dinner the predetermined recognition for meeting a production goal. You'll be amazed at how much focus and collaboration will occur. And the chances of actually achieving the goal will be increased.

> *I can live for two months on one good compliment!*
> Mark Twain

70. Invite others to "benchmark" your team. Few things send a more powerful recognition message than having others study and learn from what your group is doing. And there are two added benefits: 1) you increase the pride level within your group, and 2) you help others who gain from your experiences.

71. Consider giving day planners, personal organizers, or schedule-management software as recognition gifts. You'll do the person a great service ... and yourself as well.

72. MAKE IT A DOUBLE SHARE! Recognize someone with two of something (like cans of popcorn) – one to share with folks at work, and one to share with family at home. The gratitude for good work expands when others gain personally from it.

73. SWITCH SHOES! Nothing builds understanding and appreciation more than walking awhile in someone else's shoes (i.e., doing their job). See what the working world is like for others. You'll build empathy and trust. And you'll send the message that understanding what the individual does on a daily basis is important to you. Know what that is? It's called RECOGNITION!

74. Do you wear name tags or badges where you work? If so (and if procedures allow), recognize people with small pins and stickers they can mount on their badges. It's taking the "five-year pin" concept to a new level. And you just might find that people don't mind wearing those ID's as much as they used to!

75. GIVE THEM A "CREATURE COMFORT"! Recognize people's good work with a new chair, a fan for their office, a radio, or some other convenience that enhances their particular work space. If possible, make it their personal property that they can take with them if they transfer, are promoted, or retire.

76. Don't overlook the simple and obvious: Take the person OUT for lunch.

77. Don't be afraid to GIVE 'EM A BANANA!
(See next page)

At the Foxboro Company,
a technical advance was desperately needed
for the company to survive in its early days.

Late one evening, a scientist rushed into
the president's office with a working prototype.
It was just what they needed
to keep the business afloat.

Dumfounded at the elegance of the solution
and bemused about how to reward it, the president
bent forward in his chair, rummaged through his
desk drawers, found something,
leaned over the desk to the scientist, and said,

"Here!"

In his hand was a banana – the only reward he could
immediately put his hands on.

From that point on, the small "gold banana" pin
has been the highest accolade
for scientific achievement at Foxboro.

Adapted from
In Search of Excellence
Tom Peters and Bob Waterman
Warner Books

78. Contact a local distributor and order candy bars with customized wrappers that say things like "Thanks for going above and beyond." They're unique and fairly inexpensive – a great way to recognize those smaller daily actions that deserve some type of acknowledgment. Consider dropping the suggestions that the wrappers be saved and pinned on a bulletin board after the treat has been enjoyed.

79. Use exxxxxxxxxtra special exaggggggggggerated words in informal written communications to recognize <u>OUTSTANDING</u> results and grrrrrrrreat performance!!!!!!!

I resemble that remark!
Curly Howard

80. Establish a recognition newsletter – paper or electronic – that is distributed periodically. Ask members of your work group to recommend co-workers (and their positive performance stories) to be mentioned. And make sure you cover any fun, unique, or creative *ways* that people have been recognized.

81. ASK THEM WHAT THEY THINK! Recognize team members by asking for their ideas and inputs on work processes, future purchases, and decisions you are facing. The message: "Your opinions are valuable ... YOU are valuable."

82. Does the person you want to recognize have internet access? If so, SEND AN E-CARD! There are plenty of websites offering this free service. And if the person is "on the net" at home, consider sending the e-card there. Either way, they'll be in for a nice surprise when they see that familiar phrase: **You've Got Mail!**

83. HAVE A PICNIC! Don't wait for the official company picnic to have a get-together. Organize a small, informal, everyone-brings-something-to-share event to recognize team efforts and boost team spirit.

84. TAKE A PEER OUT FOR A ROOTBEER!

85. Commemorate the day a co-worker joined your group. Think how you'd feel receiving a simple note that said something like: *Hey Syd – In case you forgot, you came on board three years ago today. It's a date I won't forget because of your many contributions. Thanks for being such an important member of the team.*

86. If you're a supervisor or manager, have a TRUE "Open Door" Policy through which people can voice their problems and concerns to you. You don't have to agree with people in order to listen to them and consider what they have to say. Again, the message to people is: "You are important!"

87. Schedule an "agenda-less" meeting 2-3 times each year. Make the only topic: HEY, WHAT'S ON YOUR MIND? You'll demonstrate that you care. And, you'll encourage communication that leads to a high-trust environment.

88. Next time a deserving senior manager is being acknowledged by the organization – or recognized in a paper or trade journal – send a short note of congratulations.

89. SHARE *YOUR* SUCCESSES! Recognize the people who contribute to whatever *you* are recognized for.

*O*utstanding leaders

go out of their way

to boost the self-esteem

of their personnel.

If people believe in themselves,

it's amazing

what they can accomplish.

Sam Walton

90. Keep a camera (loaded with film) on hand to record special events and special people. Post the pictures in a common area. And when it's time to take them down, place them in a photo album for all to enjoy.

91. Recognize people (and teach others) by telling positive "campfire stories." Start your next meeting with something like: "Let me tell about the time Kathy and Carlos saved the day with XYZ Enterprises, our biggest customer ..."

92. Here's an often overlooked way of recognizing good performers: Address the problems of POOR performers! Letting others get away with sub-par behavior is a slap in the face to the majority of those who carry their share of the load – and more.

93. GET RID OF YOUR BEST PEOPLE! (Chill out! It's not what you think.) Do everything you can to help your good performers get promoted or receive special assignments. They'll appreciate the huge recognition, and you'll enhance your reputation. Become known as the department that develops and advances employees at all levels, and the best and brightest people will beat a path to your door.

94. When all else fails, SHUT UP! Seriously, letting others do the talking (stating opinions, asking questions, etc.) rather than you monopolizing the conversation is, in fact, a form of recognition.

95. ASK THEM TO "SUB4U"! If you're a supervisor, you can recognize people in your work group by asking them to represent you at meetings you can't attend. They'll appreciate the confidence you place in them, and they'll get to see what really goes on in "those meetings." On second thought ...

96. LEND A HAND! Tell co-workers that they can count on you for help if they ever get behind at work. And if they take you up on your offer, DELIVER!

97. PUT THEM IN CHARGE … OF SOMETHING! Sharing authority (*real* authority) is a great way to recognize people. Let your positive performers run meetings, control pieces of equipment, "own" rooms, etc. Set some general parameters, but give them a free hand in managing their piece of the organization. Just make sure that any extra work involved isn't viewed as a punishment rather than a reward!

98. As people prove themselves through achievement, designate them "our recognized expert in the area of ____." Post a master EXPERTS list in your work area. When others have questions or need assistance, send them to your "expert." Set a goal to eventually have each person in your group named as an expert of something.

99. GIVE THEM THEIR OWN TREE! Recognize a good performer by planting a tree – on company grounds – in their honor.

Going "outside the box"
(getting creative)

There are as many ways to recognize people as there are people to recognize. You just have to use your brain to find them. Next time you think you've exhausted the possibilities, THINK AGAIN ... and again!

100. SEND A RECOGNITION FAX! Using a non-traditional method of acknowledgment tends to make a big impression – especially when the person works right next to you.

101. NAME SOMETHING IN THEIR HONOR! Officially dedicating "The Karen Jones Printer" or the "Bill Lee Forklift" by affixing an inexpensive engraved brass plaque can be a fun yet powerful form of recognition. And its impact will extend well beyond the presentation ceremony.

102. GET PERSONAL! Need to recognize someone special who's leaving, transferring, or retiring? Do it with a strong personal touch. Things like a scrapbook of workplace memories, a song written and sung by the team, or a video of goodbye messages from co-workers (to name only a few) can be touching and memorable ways to say, "You will be missed."

103. Recognize someone with a paid subscription to a magazine of their choice (within certain obvious limits). The cost is minimal, and your appreciation will be reinforced with each issue they receive!

104. LET THEM CONTROL THEIR SCHEDULE! Recognize your better performers by letting them vary their lunch and break schedules (as long as the work is covered). Having the ability to adjust one's time to personal needs and desires is a valuable perk.

While we're on that subject, consider giving "the gift of time." Here are 10 examples of things you can arrange, pay for, or do that will allow folks some free time:

105. A one-time house cleaning;

106. Detailing of a car;

107. An oil change;

108. Babysitting for a night out on the town;

109. Babysitting *out*side the home (so they are free to work *in*side the home);

110. A one-time lawn service or yard manicure;

111. Extra time off for holiday shopping;

112. Laundry or cleaning services;

113. Taxi or transportation services;

114. "Handyman" services to handle a project that otherwise would take time and money … and has the potential of getting screwed up (i.e., MORE time, MORE money!).

In today's fast-paced world, free time is like GOLD!

To say "well done" to any bit of good work is to take hold of the powers which have made the effort and strengthen them beyond our knowledge.

Phillip Brooks

115. Looking to recognize someone who did great with a tough assignment? GIVE THEM AN *EASY* JOB! Beware of unintentionally punishing good performers by continually giving them really hard stuff.

116. Start a group tradition by creating a funny, tongue-in-cheek, "laugh at ourselves" award to kid good performers for humorous things (a.k.a. goofs) that happen. Start with yourself, and make sure that everyone sees it as a positive ritual.

117. Place a RECOGNITION BOX filled with cards, sticky notes, happy-face stickers, etc., in a common area. Encourage people to "go to the box" frequently to acknowledge co-workers' good performance. If the supply is readily available, there's a greater likelihood it will be used by everyone ... especially if YOU set the example.

118. ESTABLISH A "WALL OF FAME"! Post all kinds of stuff: pictures of team members, copies of certificates of completion for training, thank you notes from customers, newspaper clippings about the organization's success, etc. Let your creativity flow ... and be sure to solicit ideas from your colleagues.

119. Recognize someone with a hardbound book on a favorite subject or by a favorite author (autographed would be a special touch). Write your recognition message inside the front cover. The person will be "re-recognized" every time they pick it up and read your words.

120. Make and deliver someone's early morning coffee. And make sure you associate your action with their good performance (e.g., "You've done such a great job lately with the scheduling, I wanted to help you get a great start on today.")

121. Create fun awards to give in addition to regular, more serious recognition. Example: Give "The Big Kahuna" Award" – complete with *big kahuna headdress* to wear – for being tops in sales, or for having the best new idea of the year. And when you bestow such awards, CELEBRATE!

122. SEND POSTCARDS! Even in today's *cyber*world, people still like to receive picture postcards. And they appreciate knowing others are thinking of them. So next time you're away on business (or even on vacation) drop a card in the mail. It doesn't need to be long or fancy – a simple "Best Wishes to a Great Team" can have a big impact for a minimal investment.

123. HAVE 'EM DO IT THEMSELVES! Ask your team members to develop their own recognition program. Give them a budget, some general parameters, and a bunch of support. You'll not only get recognition ideas that are appreciated and supported, but you'll also get people involved in enhancing the work environment. That's a great "double hit"!

124. LET THEM "SIGN THEIR WORK"! Recognize high quality performers by allowing them to sign or initial their work or include a small "I Made This" note or tag. Consider providing contact information so customers can pass along their reactions to the product or service directly to the person who did the work.

125. PUT THEIR NAME UP IN LIGHTS! Next time a colleague is traveling on business, call ahead to their hotel and see if you can get it to display a welcome on its outside marquee (or hotel information TV channel). Example: "Welcome Pat Smith, Best Boss Award Winner!"

126. CREATE A "PASS-ALONG AWARD" … some sort of trophy, gizmo, stuffed animal, etc., that has meaning to the group. Include some pass-along rules, like: "The 'Stuffed Monkey Award' (*no monkey business here*) for quality performance must be passed along by the recipient to another deserving person within two weeks of receipt." Let everyone contribute to the type of award(s) and accompanying rules.

127. Here's another fun way to recognize someone who's leaving your work group: RETIRE THEIR "JERSEY"! You've seen sports teams do it. Why shouldn't you? Get an old work shirt, company shirt, t-shirt, or whatever the person might have been known for wearing. Put their name on it, mount it on a framed bulletin board, add an inexpensive engraved plaque, and you're ready to hang it in a permanent workplace location … and to celebrate!

> *There are two things people want more than sex and money – recognition and praise!*
> Mary Kay Ash

128. AWARD GOLD STARS! Don't underestimate the power of this carry-over from school days. You can use the paper stick-ons, or candy gold stars, or have lapel pins made. Will some folks think it's corny? Sure … but only until the competition to see who gets the most of those "silly little stars" kicks in!

129. Do you have an electronic scrolling message board in your cafeteria (or other common area)? If so, USE IT to recognize people in your work group. Arrange for a small congratulatory blurb to run for at least 2 days.

130. Implement a THREE STROKES AND YOU'RE OUT policy through which people in your work group get a half day off after receiving three commendations from customers.

131. If your organization supports charities, consider making some of the donations in the name of an employee you wish to recognize. Better yet, allow the individual to select which charity will receive the money in her or his name.

132. Declare a "we deserve candy" break and give everyone a treat from your PEZ dispenser. What? You don't have one? Well ... GET ONE! In fact, get one for *everyone* in your work group and encourage them to "PEZ each other" whenever they see something worthy of immediate recognition.

133. Want to recognize someone who happens to be a sports fanatic? Consider arranging for a pay-per-view (the company pays) of a special event they can enjoy in the comfort of their home. You might even get invited!

134. GIVE THEM RECOGNITION BUTTONS! All you need is a button/badge maker (about $150), a computer with a color printer, and a little imagination, and you'll be set to give out recognition that people can wear proudly. Have fun devising button slogans such as: "I'm a Customer Service SUPER Star!"

135. GIVE THEM PLAY MONEY –
in various amounts that match the significance of the performance recognized. The money is saved and eventually "cashed in" for free lunches, time off, special perks, etc.

*T*he highest compliments
leaders can receive
are those that are given
by the people who work for them.

James L. Barksdale

A Note to Every Employee

Dear Employee:
  I admit it – I need to do a better job of giving
  you the recognition you deserve. I DO appreciate
  your efforts and contributions, and I'll work
  harder at showing it more often.
  As I work on that, maybe you could look for an
  occasional opportunity to recognize ME! After
  all, bosses want and need recognition, too. And
  we usually get even less than employees do.
  Like you, I want to feel good about myself and
  what I do – and YOU can help. Remember that
  recognizing your boss is not about "kissing up,"
  it's about extending the same courtesy
  you wish to receive yourself.

Every Manager

136. THEY OUTTA BE IN PICTURES! Next time your organization takes pictures for an ad or brochure, or makes a promotional video, arrange for a team member to "star" in the production. Just make sure that they perceive it as a plus.

137. Ask your co-workers what they would like you to bring back (brochures, information, a book, etc.) from your next trade show or business trip.

138. Recognize an individual or group with a batch of cookies that you bake yourself. It won't take long for the word to spread: "If you get cookies from (your name), you know you've done well."

139. Let people pick their own semi-official titles like: Guru of Quality, Queen of Customer Service, CyberWizard, etc. Use these titles in informal, inner-company correspondence.

140. GET 'EM BUSINESS CARDS! For people who normally don't have or use cards, this is a super high-impact form of recognition. Consider allowing them to put special titles (#139, above) on the cards. Then sit back and watch them smile as they're re-recognized each time they give a card to someone.

141. GIVE THEM THEIR OWN DAY! Recognize special people by declaring a future work date as *their* day. For example: "Next Thursday is Martha Lopez Day!" Arrange a small party. Give them a commemorative certificate. And ask everyone in your work group to say or do something to contribute to the celebration.

142. Want to recognize your team for taking on a tough and stressful project? Bring in a certified professional to give in-office, stress-relieving neck and shoulder massages.

143. KEEP A "LEARNING LOG." Use a small notebook or dedicate pages in your day planner to record recognition ideas you want to implement. Jot down things you hear, read, or observe in others – including ideas you "borrow" from other businesses. Scan your log at the beginning of each week as a reminder of ways you can acknowledge the efforts and contributions of your co-workers.

144. If you come across an article in a magazine or newspaper that may be of interest to a co-worker, pass it along with a short recognition note. Example: "Pat, I remember your comment about improving our time management. Well, here's an article that supports your ideas." Not only are you passing along a helpful resource, you're also sending a powerful message that what the person has to say is important.

145. BE AN ED KOCH! The former mayor of New York City would routinely walk the streets of the city, approach people, and say: "Hi there. I'm Mayor Ed Koch. How am I doing?" By asking others for their opinions and feedback, you're extending a gesture of respect – the cornerstone of effective recognition. And, you'll walk away with some pretty helpful feedback to enhance your own performance.

146. MULTIPLY THE MOMENT! Take a picture of a co-worker being recognized. Have the photo enlarged, frame it, and give it to the person as a gift … and an additional form of recognition. *(See #90)*

According to a survey by Robert Half International Inc., **as many as 25% of good employees who quit their jobs cite a lack of appreciation as their reason.**

147. Welcome a co-worker back from vacation with an update on the status of activities, projects, goals, etc. You'll send the message that the person is an important part of the organization who needs to know what's happening.

148. GIVE TABLE SERVICE! Arrange for a dessert, a special beverage, or just a nice thank you note to be sent to a co-worker while they're at dinner on a business trip. This is especially impressive if they're dining with a customer or a senior manager.

149. Create theme awards to recognize noteworthy achievers. Examples: "The Juggler Award" for the person able to handle the most competing priorities, or "The Slim Pickens Award" for the best budget stretcher.

SPEAKING FOR THE COMPANY

1-800-FLOWERS is a $300 million business, and one of the reasons is its leader's dedication to motivating his employees. CEO Jim McCann uses candy and theater tickets to reward and energize team members. He also offers one other unusual and powerful perk: the opportunity to speak on behalf of the company. Look for venues where your employees can spread the word about your organization, and their enthusiasm and passion for their work will grow dramatically.

The Motivational Manager

150. GIVE 'EM $2.00 BILLS! Yes, they're still made, and they're available at most banks. Put them in a frame along with a mini-certificate of commendation. This uncommon denomination can be a good way to recognize uncommon performance.

151. CREATE A QUIET PLACE! To recognize "the whole person" that works with you, you must acknowledge "the whole person" realities in their lives. A quiet place, where people can enjoy a few private moments while at work, will be a godsend for everyone from stressed workers to nursing mothers.

152. When you have position openings, ask your better performers to get actively involved in the recruitment process. If possible, make it a special assignment. The message: "You're one of our very best people. You know what it takes to be successful here. Help us find more folks like YOU!"

153. MAKE THEM "CO-AUTHORS"! Involve people you want to recognize in developing a training manual. Example: "High-Impact Customer Service Techniques, by members of the ABC Sales Team." Make sure each contributor is listed as a co-author in the credits.

154. Ask your computer gurus to help you create a recognition SCREEN SAVER to honor a special performer. Include a photograph of the honoree as well as messages from folks in your work group.

155. HAVE 'EM GIVE YOU FIVE! Ask team members to give you five ideas for "making this a better place to work for all of us." Make a real effort to implement at least one thing from their list. And make sure the appropriate person gets credit for the idea.

*I*t's not enough
to merely believe in recognition.
You also have to *BEHAVE*
like you believe in it!

156. Create the equivalent of a "game ball" – an object (it could actually be a ball) signed by each team member and given to the person designated by the team as the MVP for each completed project.

157. EXCHANGE AMBASSADORS! Visit other departments and have them visit you. You'll recognize the people you send AND the ones that stay behind to serve as hosts or guides for your visitors.

158. GIVE 'EM A KAZOO SALUTE! Seriously! Give a kazoo to everyone on your team and periodically recognize people with a group salute. Better yet, play them a kazoo koncerto!

159. Recognize someone with a "mini-scholarship" to attend an educational or personal development activity of their choosing, with no strings (i.e., job-related requirements) attached.

160. GIVE OUT TOOTSIE ROLL® POPS! They're fun, come in different flavors, cost next to nothing, and offer a way to give immediate recognition for small contributions. Think this one is meaningless? Try it for a while and then stop. I guarantee that some good performer will express disappointment for not getting a Tootsie Pop.

161. GIVE 'EM A NAME! Recognize your team with a special descriptive name (e.g., "The Technowizards" or "The Service Aces"). Better yet, let them pick their own name. Then hang a large banner in your work area that says:

Home of The (team name)

162. Recognize a co-worker by showing up at their child's soccer game, school play, or other event. They'll appreciate your interest. And if asked why you're there, you can say, "I just wanted to see if your kid is as good a performer as you are!"

163. Recognize people who "walk the talk" with a pair of toy chattering teeth. Suggest that the teeth be passed along to others they see practicing organizational values.

164. Say thanks with an emergency car kit – one that includes jumper cables, flashlight, flares, flat-fixer, and a few tools. Throw in a $10 bill (just in case it's needed). For people that are important to you, this recognition could be a life saver ... LITERALLY!

Recognition Checklist

Make sure the recognition you provide is:

☐ **TIMELY**

Don't wait. Give recognition as soon as possible after the good performance takes place. Praise tends to lose its effectiveness with the passing of time.

☐ **SPECIFIC**

Tell the person exactly what they did that was good. A mere "nice job" really doesn't say all that much. Being specific lets the person know what behaviors to repeat in the future.

☐ **SINCERE**

Insincere praise is usually worse than none at all. Be honest and open. Tell the person what their performance means to you personally.

☐ **INDIVIDUAL**

Focus on individuals rather than groups. Fact is, not all team members contribute equally.

☐ **PERSONAL**

Adjust the style and method of your recognition to the receiver. Some people like public praise, some prefer private discussions. Give "different strokes to different folks." Not sure what they prefer? Ask!

☐ **PROPORTIONAL**

Match the amount and intensity of recognition to the achievement. Going overboard for small stuff will make people question your motives.

165. Give a "passport" card for a day off to be used any time during the year (with advance approval, of course).

166. SEND 'EM TO THE CHEST! Keep a treasure chest with an assortment of recognition items like caps, mugs, movie tickets, video rental certificates, etc. Consider including a "biggie" like an envelope with a $100 bill inside. When someone deserves a special acknowledgment for positive performance, let them reach into the chest and pick a surprise.

167. Declare a "Positive Feedback Day" during which negatives are underplayed and good news and appreciation flows.

168. SEND "PASS-ALONG" FLOWERS! Attach a routing slip (with instructions) to a bouquet of fresh flowers for your work team. Each person keeps the flowers for a half day and then passes them along to the next name  on the slip. After everyone has had a turn, the flowers are placed in a common area for all to enjoy.

169. Like to reward someone who's about to embark on a long and tedious business trip? Upgrade him or her to a first-class plane seat. Or, arrange for a rental car or hotel room upgrade. Better yet, do ALL of them!!

170. "Spring" for memberships in professional associations, discount buying clubs, local YMCAs, etc.

> *You like me. You really like me!*
> Sally Field

171. TAKE 'EM FOR A RIDE! Arrange for a co-worker to ride along with the plant manager on her or his weekly facility tour, or ride along with a service technician to visit a customer, or the like. "Ride-alongs" represent learning experiences, opportunities to develop relationships with others, and chances to do something different at work.

172. Think about a good performing co-worker. Make a list of a dozen things you like, appreciate, admire, or respect about the person. Then, GO TELL THEM! Be specific as you share this feedback. The person will be better for it ... and so will you!

173. Create "You Deserve a Hand" cards for customers and peers to recognize members of your work group. Make sure the cards have space for a small description note and a place for the giver's signature. Distribute the cards with instructions. Receivers accumulate the cards and eventually trade them for gifts, perks, or time off.

174. GIVE THEM MEDALS! Have a team that's worked hard on a special project or landed a big account? When the "campaign" is over and the "battle" won, give everyone a "medal of merit and heroism." Consider having a special ceremony and invite a high-ranking "officer" to make the presentations.

175. While we're on the subject ... have a large poster of a medal printed and laminated. Put it in a common area and add the names and achievements of people you want to recognize.

176. Make MVP "trading cards" for your team members. Include a photograph, position (job), specific achievements, and some personal information (e.g., hobbies) on each. Post them in a common area and make sure everyone gets a copy.

177. TURN 'EM INTO RINGERS! Install a big metal bell, in a common area, to be rung in celebration of individual or group achievements. Anyone can ring the bell – which is everyone's cue to assemble, hear the good news, and celebrate!

178. SPONSOR AN OPEN HOUSE! Remember how proud you were when family and friends came to visit your school and see your work? Why not recreate that same pride by giving your co-workers' family and friends a similar opportunity? Recognize the members of your team by inviting the people they care about to come and see where they work and what they do. It's a great chance for everyone to show off a little.

179. Create "organizational immortality" for that VERY special person. Name a location, facility, or event after them. Examples: Dedicate "The Walter Johnson Cafeteria" in honor of the 30-year retiring employee or "The Carolyn Kravitz Leadership Conference" for the recently promoted department head.

and finally ...

180. When all is said and done, using the very best behavioral science research techniques known to mankind, the absolute best and most surefire way to know how to recognize the people who are important to you and to your organization is ...

...GO ASK THEM!

And as you find out, jot down those ideas here:

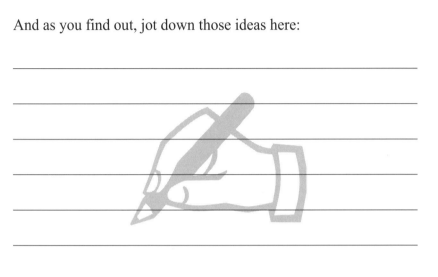

A closing thought ...

Nine-tenths of wisdom
is APPRECIATION.
Go find somebody's hand
          and squeeze it ...
while there's still time!

Dale Dauten

About The WALK THE TALK® Company!

Since 1977, **The WALK THE TALK Company** has helped individuals and organizations, worldwide, achieve success through Values-Based Practices. Our goal is both simple and straightforward: **to provide you and your organization with high-impact resources for your personal and professional success!**

We specialize in ...
- "How-To" Handbooks and Support Material
- Video Training Programs
- Inspirational Gift Books and Movies
- Do-It-Yourself Training Resources
- Motivational Newsletters
- 360° Feedback Processes
- The Popular *Start Right...Stay Right* and *Santa's Leadership Secrets*™ Product Line *And much more!*

**To learn more about our full range of WALK THE TALK® resources,
please visit us at www.walkthetalk.com
or
To speak to one of our Customer Service Representatives,
Please call 1.888.822.9255**

About The Author

Eric Harvey is president and founder of WalkTheTalk.com. For over thirty years, Eric and his team have helped thousands of organizations and individuals, worldwide, achieve success throug Ethical Leadership and Values-Based Practices. Eric is a renowne speaker, business consultant, and coauthor of thirty highly acclai books, including the best-selling *WALK THE TALK...And Get The Results You Want, Ethics4Everyone,* and *The Leadership Secrets Santa Claus.*

WALKTHETALK.COM

Resources for Personal and Professional Success

ONLY $79.95!

Program

This high-impact "do-it-yourself" program includes:

✓ Leaders Guide with instructions, learning exercises, preparation suggestions, and other training tips.

✓ PowerPoint training visuals which can easily be customized to fit your audience and training objectives.

For only **$79.95**, you can train your entire team on the key concepts found in the book. Once you order, you will receive instructions via email on how to download the complete *180 Ways to Walk the Recognition UTrain Program*. It's that easy! Please make sure you include your email address on the order form when you order.

Also consider...
The
LEADERSHIP DEVELOPMENT
LIBRARY

Contains 13 best-selling books...all designed to help you and your team achieve success in leadership.

SAVE OVER 30%

ONLY $99.95

For more information, visit www.walkthetalk.com, or call toll-free 1.888.822.9255

☑ **Please send me extra copies of:** *180 Ways To Walk The Recognition Talk*

1-99 copies $9.95 each   100-499 copies $8.95 each   500+ copies please call

---

180 Ways To Walk The Recognition Talk   _____ copies X   _____   =$_____

Other WALK THE TALK Resources

180 Ways To Walk The Recognition Talk UTrain   _____ sets X $ 79.95   =$_____

The Leadership Development Library   _____ sets X $ 99.95   =$_____

Product Total	$_____
*Shipping & Handling	$_____
Subtotal	$_____
Sales Tax:	
Texas Sales Tax – 8.25%	$_____
CA Sales/Use Tax	$_____
Total (U.S. Dollars Only)	$_____

(Sales & Use Tax Collected on TX & CA Customers Only)

*Shipping and Handling Charges

No. of Books	1-4	5-9	10-24	25-49	50-99	100-199	200+
Total Shipping	$6.75	$10.95	$17.95	$26.95	$48.95	$84.95	$89.95+$0.25/book

Call 972.899.8300 for quote if outside continental U.S. Orders are shipped ground delivery 3-5 business days.
Next and 2nd business day delivery available – call 888.822.9255.

Name_____   Title_____

Organization_____

Shipping Address_____
City_____ (No PO Boxes) _____ State_____ Zip _____

Phone_____   Fax_____

E-Mail_____

Charge Your Order: ❑ MasterCard   ❑ Visa   ❑ American Express

Credit Card Number_____ Exp. Date_____

❑ Check Enclosed (Payable to The WALK THE TALK Company)

❑ Please Invoice (**Orders over $250 ONLY**)   P.O. Number (required) _____

WALKTHETALK.COM
Resources for Personal and Professional Success

PHONE	ONLINE	MAIL
PHONE 1.888.822.9255 or 972.899.8300 M-F, 8:30-5:00 Cen.	**ONLINE** www.walkthetalk.com **FAX** 972.899.9291	**MAIL** WalkTheTalk.com 1100 Parker Square, Suite 25 Flower Mound, TX 75028

Prices effective September 2007 are subject to change.